Flamingo
Coloring Book

Get FREE printable coloring pages and discounted book prices sent straight to your e-mail inbox every week!

Sign up at:
www.adultcoloringworld.net

Copyright © 2016 Adult Coloring World
All rights reserved.
ISBN-13: 978-1530598922
ISBN-10: 1530598923

Previews:

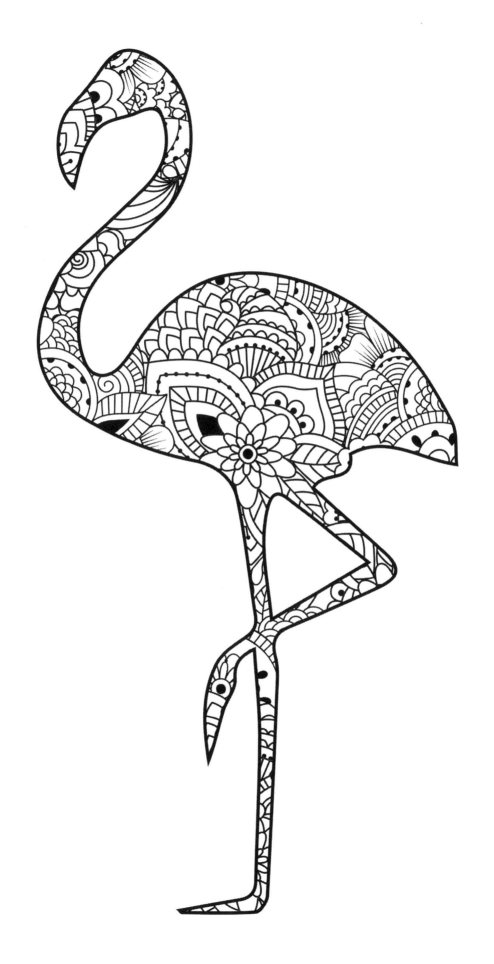

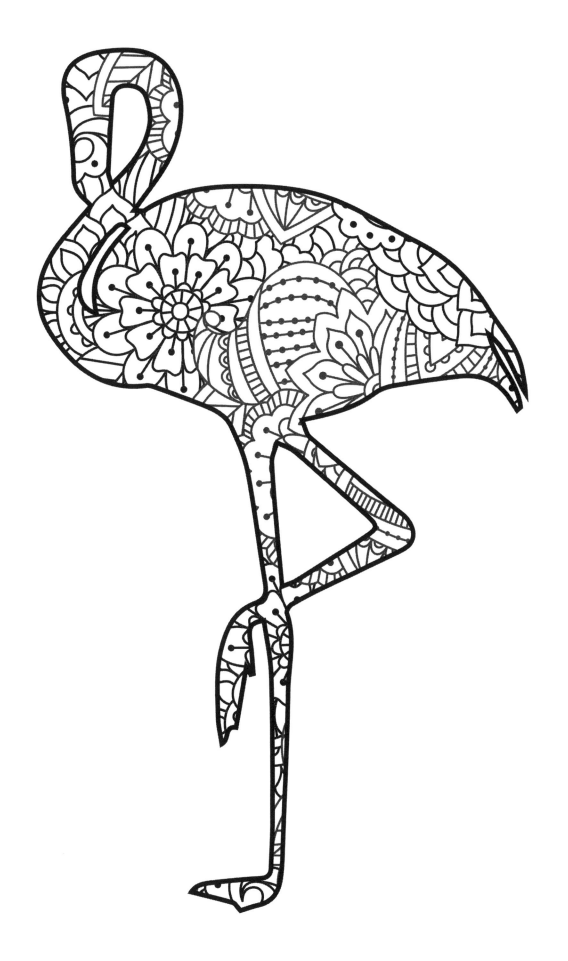

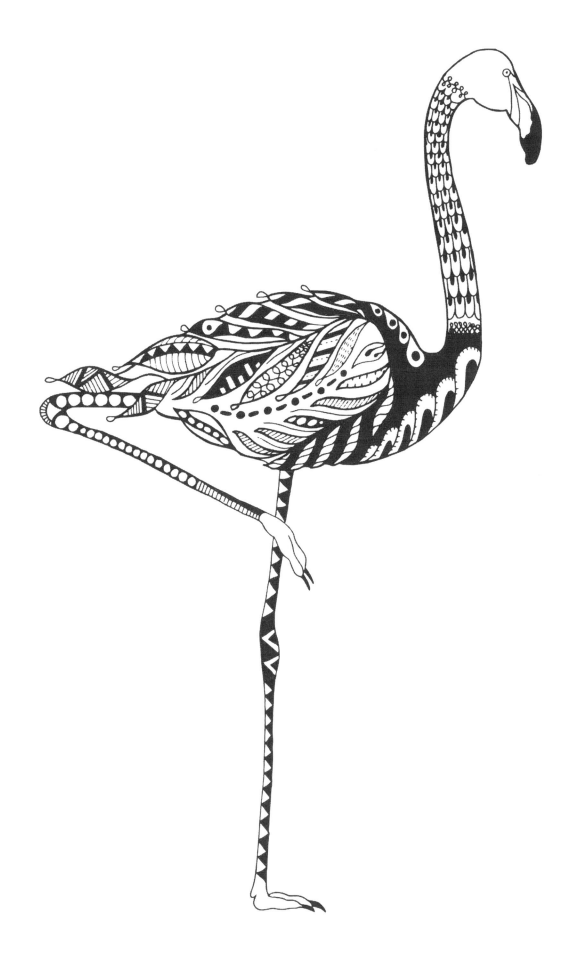

Color Test Page

Color Test Page

Made in the USA
San Bernardino, CA
14 March 2017